Rock Woman At Rest

*To Dave -
Once a teacher,
always a teacher.
Sincere Regards,
[signature]*

Rock Woman At Rest

Poetry and Writing by Dawn Marie Nevills

iUniverse, Inc.
New York Lincoln Shanghai

Rock Woman At Rest

Copyright © 2005 by Dawn Marie Nevills

All rights reserved. No part of this book may be used or reproduced by any means, graphic, electronic, or mechanical, including photocopying, recording, taping or by any information storage retrieval system without the written permission of the publisher except in the case of brief quotations embodied in critical articles and reviews.

iUniverse books may be ordered through booksellers or by contacting:

iUniverse
2021 Pine Lake Road, Suite 100
Lincoln, NE 68512
www.iuniverse.com
1-800-Authors (1-800-288-4677)

ISBN-13: 978-0-595-35176-3 (pbk)
ISBN-13: 978-0-595-79875-9 (ebk)
ISBN-10: 0-595-35176-X (pbk)
ISBN-10: 0-595-79875-6 (ebk)

Printed in the United States of America

(Dedicated, with love, to Nico and Julianna)

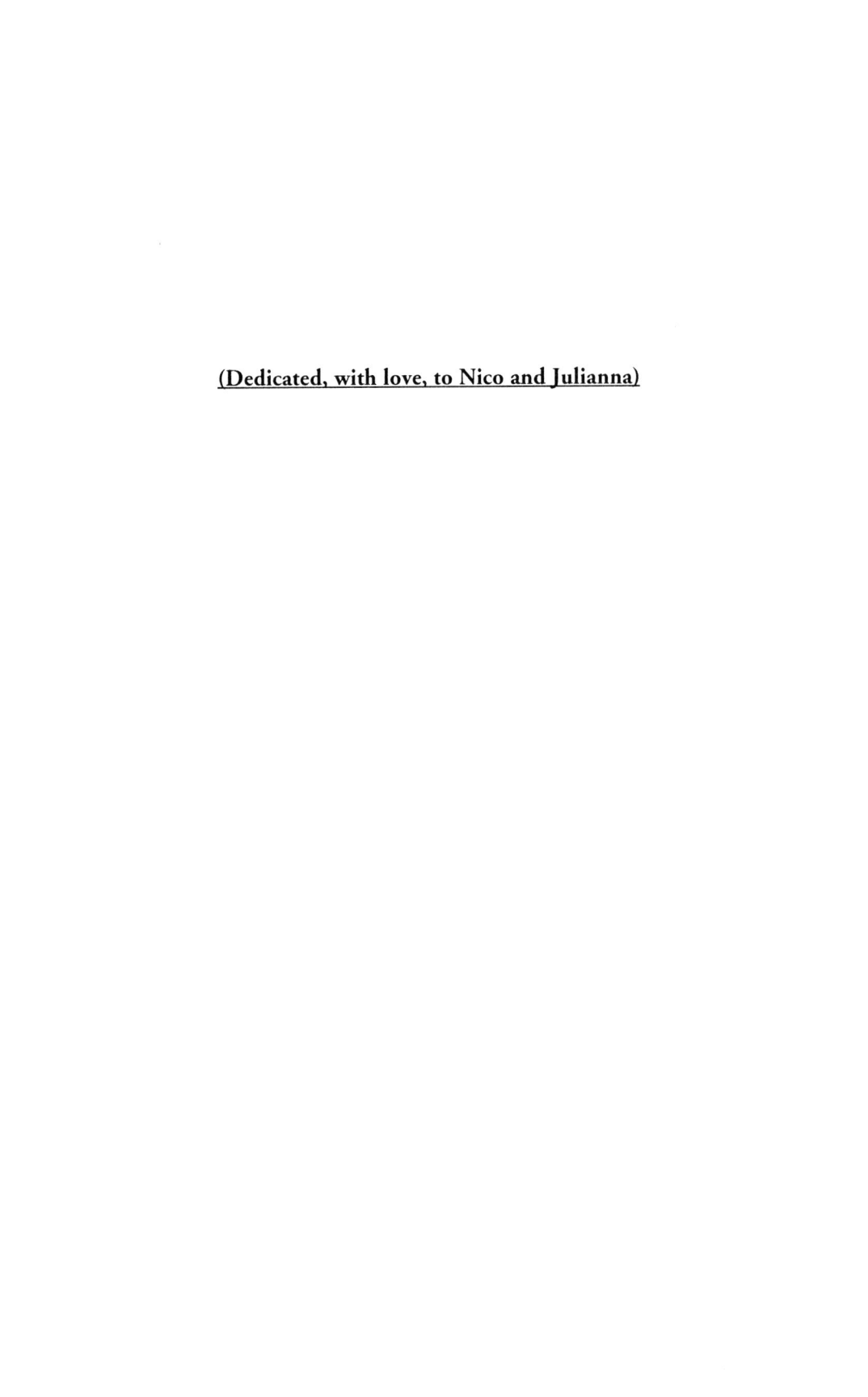

Contents

Section 1 1

Spring, Beneath this blanket of winter, warm and waiting 2
Lines in Praise of Poetry 3
to each his own 4
Speaking beyond the speed of sound 5
Running up that road 7
Moving Forward 8
Clown's Feet 9
Big Top Memories 10
Woman 13
What will your gift be, this year? 14
The one to tell you 15
A moment remembered 17

Section 2 19

Poems Written in Korea 19
April 1997 20
April 25, 1997 21
April 25, 1997 22
May 13, 1997 24
May 24, 1997 A harbour recital in Pusan 26
Friday, June 6, 1997 Seaside Storytelling 27

On Buddhists 28

To men angry and afraid 30

Untitled 32

Celebrating Singspiel's victory (of the Triple Crown) with genuine affection and good humour after watching it, on CNN 33

Section 3: "A Return to Sender" 35

Coming Home 36

On love and hate 38

On-line farming 39

Musical accompaniment 40

Toronto Arrival 41

The secret sock (a joke with the Pope) 45

The Weather's fine 46

Building Blocks 47

Morning Puffs (looking at the stacks, watchfully, while working at Esso) . . 49

More-Musical Accompaniment 50

Descriptive sign at war memorial 51

My poems: for me, they spell "the rap…y?" (Scene:Ipperwash/Azhoodena) . 52

Living near water 53

Runway Romance (a late birthday gift) 54

Penny Lover 55

Syntactical Discourse 56

Time passes 57

I have a kind of spatial mind 58

The moon is full, this civic day, and I must travel 59

Sing, gai jing! 60

In praise of jazz 61

A poem about racism 62

Small tears	63
These grey days	64
My Friend Jennie	65
Dancing for Ribbons	66
At the Carnival	67
My canine companion	69
(Part 2—Return from Comatose—"The Brandy Bark")	71

Section 4: The Brothers Grim m ... 73

The untouchables	74
Sometimes	76
Everything old is new again…an ode to recycling	77
Burdens	78

Section 5: Love Poems ... 79

Untitled	80
About socks	81
Gaze glazing	82
Explained depths	83
Portrait of a filled sweater	84
A whale of a thought…	85
A poem here	86
A poem there	87
Sandbox silliness	88

Section 6: Bean talkin' to) the impossible One" ... 93

Because of Rowin A. (addered up)	94
Petals aglow woo	96

Wonkbonkered thusly (Farmerknighted) 97
Banilla 98
Style rhymes timed protection 99
On Buddha and Mountaintops 100
Diagram of above poem 101
A shock of progress 102
The Fellowship (A merry vessel) 103
Our daily trek 104
In praise of my hero, Shakespeare (simple elogy) (…whilst enthroned) . . . 105
The Night Progresses 107
Briefly Metaphorical Feelines 108
My Thing is My Own 109
Deep plain maquillage (religious meanderings) 110
P.(.oem) and (S).tructure OWNED 111
The welcome of the Quiet Door 112
Inside 113
October, 2003 114
SNAPSHOT—Wooden Sentinel 115
A "Protection" poem, custom-wise…. 116

The Administrative Years—A retrospective 117

Rhymes in Time 118
Today's Woman 119

The College Street Apartment 121

Musings upon the Wildflowers in the Back Parking Lot 122
Untitled 123
Wind's song 124

A dog's life 125

The Renaissance Man 126

A Brief Sonata on Interior Decorating, in several movements 127

"Peas", she said. 128

On carpet deodorizer 129

Watford Days **131**

An afternoon with a winged waif (for Norm and Cindy) 132

Words after a tutoring session 133

The small sentinels 134

On vegetables (an angry response to elder abuse) 136

Part one: Potatoes 137

Part two: Zucchini 138

Part three: Broccoli 139

Part four: Cauliflower 140

Creative Cover letters I really wanted to send **141**

sign posted on tree with small axe 145

Uninspired 147

A Knight Returns (A Poem for old Lovers) 148

Section 1

Spring, Beneath this blanket of winter, warm and waiting

Beneath this blanket of white, lies spring in wait;
Stretching, yawning, waiting to dance its lovely colours
Underneath the warmth of the sun.
The hand of God that maketh all things possible—
all things wonderful, in their way,
Turns each season on this wondrous medicine wheel of life,
And wind, and more life, and seeds of love,
Like gentle protectors, lead us on into another day.

Lines in Praise of Poetry

Oh, poetry, I find in thee, a vehicle to make me free,
and in your lines I can opine, a few sad words.
In saying so, and working, (though a few tossed words go to and fro
As small, tense thoughts upon a muted page),
I can begin, those words within, to hold my chin
And weather others thrown my way.
So, sweet, soft lines, which others find, as just a kind
of therapy for waning verve,
I'll try to write (but not be trite) beginning flight—
And not forget my nerve,
Especially at the start, and at the close, of each new day.

to each his own

To each his own;
For some
To teach;
For some
To sing;
For some
To reach;
For some
To wing;
For some
To write;
For some
To fight
And others…
Play.

Speaking beyond the speed of sound

I must speak for the ones who protect
So that they have a voice
Although they rarely speak
That they may feel, and grieve
And walk in front
And around
And behind
Watching, Walking
Watching, Walking
Never for a moment
Not watching, and walking
So that they watch and walk
Even when they're not watching and walking
Because their lives
Become
Watching and walking.
There is room for nothing else, ever
Only a kind of blending in of normal
Life
in order to somehow preserve
Their need
And requirement
For the sanity
Of the
Mundane.
And when their weeping comes, if it comes
it is a silent scream
A racking, gut-wrenching sob
With no sound
Only movement drawn

From
That
Watching and Walking
Which does not show
Upon the face;
But, for a breath,
Is released—
this pain of
Silent friends.

Running up that road

As I look at the laneway stretching in front of me
It might as well be the sky, sometimes;
I am a jet, I am a tank, I am a huge ship in my mind at these moments,
And I strain to overcome this body that won't move fast enough, or fluidly enough,
or with as much grace as I would like.
I imagine I am like some military ballerina, doing my pirouette, before I take that
First step on to the gravel.
There is no pain.
I walk it off.

Moving Forward

There is only one direction
There is only one focus
There is only one moment
When
Pain of Heart
Pain of Mind
Pain of Pain
Holds you in its temporary vice
Like an icy brick on your face
On your head

In front of you, blocking, rudely, your progress.
You overcome.
You move into your dreams.
Whatever might still be behind you,
Is on its own:
Cutting loose means
Treading water,
And winning.

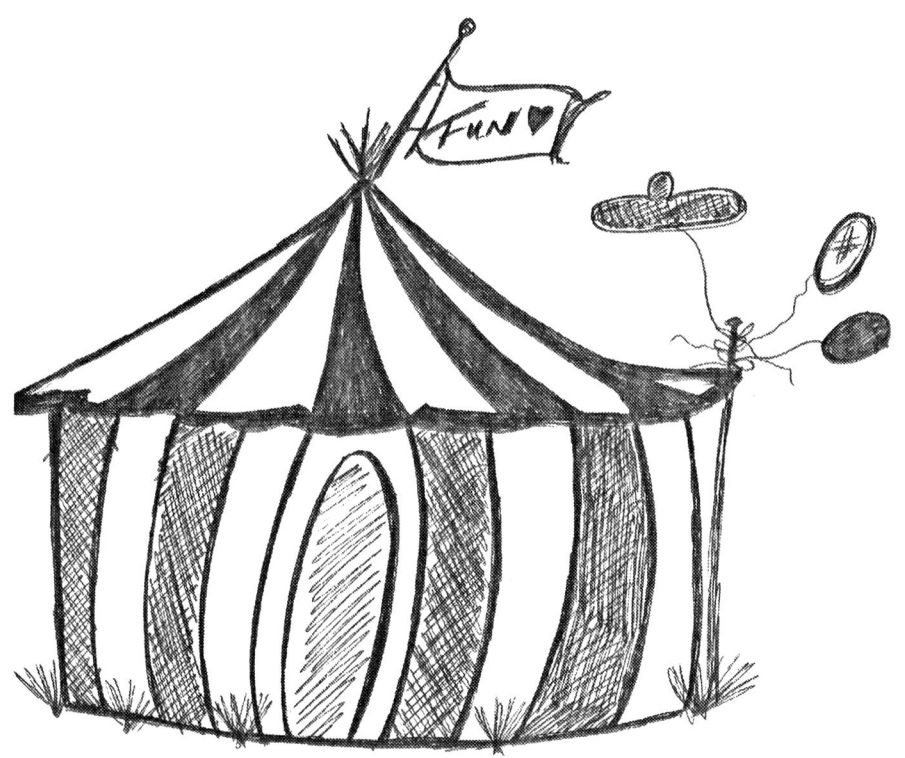

Illustration 2 "Big Top Fun"   Pen and ink   by Dawn Marie Nevills

<u>Clown's Feet</u>

For here they are,
Just like before:
(They number two,
Instead of four)
And though you sit on comfy seat—
I bet you'd stand on these clown feet!

Big Top Memories

I can remember when I was just a little girl
Playing hide and seek—was just after my Boppa died,
And, to deal with the grief I felt,
Crystal and Sylvia and I
Played "ghost hide and seek" in the trees and rosebushes
In front of my Nana's house on Holton Avenue in Hamilton, Ontario;
Laura Lee's mother, recovering from another bruising work week,
Allowed her to play, that day,
And we dreamed about having five dollars, and going down to the Big Top Restaurant
On Main Street—around the corner three blocks down—for a milkshake and some fries;
Simple wishes from kids struggling to understand life. Five dollars—a small fortune to us.
It got hot in the afternoon, and, being kids, we stripped down to our undies and
Ran through the sprinklers of the two old ladies next door
(Much to their shock and dismay).
We hadn't discovered shame of our nipples and pubis, yet,
And, even if we had, we weren't worried that some dirty old bastard
Might be getting off, watching us.
It was just so great, running through that water;
It washed away all of the things we didn't want to understand, yet,
And it seemed to me that Laura Lee loved it best—
But maybe that was just me, being sensitive; she always seemed just a little
Older, and sadder, somehow,
And it took some amount of coaxing from Nana
To get her to laugh, and run in her briefs,
Through that cooling water.
We always got a mild scolding from my Nana, when we yelled too loud, with glee;
She quietly sat on the porch, rocking,

And smiling, as she delicately arranged a few flowers
From that glorious garden that seemed so unexpected,
In the midst of those funny little wartime houses,
In a glowing old vase.
Then she'd light up a smoke, it dangling, trucker-like, from the corner of her mouth,
Silently growling "fuck off" to herself (thinking we couldn't hear, or lip read)
As the two cranky old women
Next door started whining
About
Trampled grass.
We, exhausted and replete in the tiny front yard, and shaking our wet heads like
Olympic swimmers, uncapped,
Smiled secretly back at her eloquence,
just barely overheard, as usual…..she got away with a lot like that, I think.

(Such savage elegance/eloquence the woman had….)
She must have been a fierce beauty in her day;
Somehow, we always felt an odd
Protectiveness about her.
Later, I learned that the conversations between her, and my "Toronto Aunt Bette",
(Overheard and only remembered fondly, in later years),
Validated that strength about her,
and these days,
I have my own pin, and my own secrets….
(and I, too, have been known to mouth the odd swear word under my breath,
smiling, although I haven't smoked in years)
I like to think, that at moments like this
She quietly puts her arms around me, like some comforting shawl,
And hums in my ear.
It helps to think that, when I muse on all of the things that I
Haven't quite yet, managed
to do.

And I like to think she turns from doing that, and scolds my Grandpa Mackey,
smiling,
While Boppa shakes his head, rolls his eyes, and grumbles about the skyrocketing price of
a simple popsicle for everyone, from the local Becker's store.
In heaven (complaining that more than a nickle apiece was child cruelty), he slips
the counter girl a tip…..
While
The Big Man—jolly giant Mackey—his eyes watering and his face turning purple,
from trying not to laugh—
Quietly pats him on the arm,
and mutters something about
"Terrible, this inflation".
Nana roars with laughter, (knocking a few angels' halos askew)
stopping for a moment with a raised eyebrow to say,
"Jimmy, do you not recall the conversation we had about
Underestimating Yorkshire Roses?
They, like laughter, grow everywhere…"

(No one needs to know that I only ever managed to get
One place setting—except you!)

Woman

Thrill me, fill me,
Till me, tank me.
Build me, guild me,
Mill me, bank me.
Hold me, scold me,
Fold me, thank me.
Poke me, stoke me,
Rope me, yank me,
Fork me, stork me,
Frill me, rank me.
And when thee's done,
Forget to
S
a
n k
WEEEEEEEEEEEEEEEEEEEEEEEEEEEEEEEEEEEEEEEEEEE
EEEEEEEeee.

What will your gift be, this year?

What will your gift be, this year?
Oh, not the one you'll be receiving,
But the one that you give, despite your lack of higher math;
(Doesn't seem to interfere with your capacity as a bank teller....but that's digression)
Will you give words, or actions?
Will you save a hand, or shake one?
Will you bleed, or give some?
Will you stand your ground, and speak, or will you trod upon someone else, as they struggle for
Words?
Will you stop the shot, or will you fire it?
Would you stand in front of it, to allow that person to finish their speech?
We are given choices, you and I,
About the gifts that we give.
Someone else will worry about the value of them, in the end.

<u>The one to tell you</u>

"I'm sorry for your loss"
"I'm sorry that you're devastated"
"I'm sorry to inform you"
"I'm sorry to have to be here, at this moment"
"I'm sorry to have to deliver this letter to you"
"I'm sorry to advise you"
"I'm sorry to have to watch you grieve, and feel inadequate"
"I'm sorry that your son is lying in a pile of guts on the pavement"
"I'm sorry that your beautiful daughter is mashed against the windshield of a car"
"I'm sorry that we couldn't identify the pool of human insides that used to be the person you loved"
"I'm sorry that this person will never be the same again, because of this empty bottle in the back seat"
"I'm sorry this child does not know the meaning of innocence, anymore"
"I'm sorry to have to stand beside this weeping messenger, to tell you…"
(since this person can't)
That sorry doesn't cut it, anymore.
Sorry doesn't put back the once beautiful face, because of "just one more" shot of whatever.
Sorry doesn't put back the brains inside the well-formed, could-have-been-a-doctor skull, as the result of politics, bad direction, and trigger fingers.
Sorry doesn't stop that child from screaming "please, stop" in their sleep
Sorry doesn't make that man, with his brush cut and his fatigues,
Stop crying.
I'm sorry to have to be the one to tell you, dear—
But it's my duty.
Now, forgive me if I continue knitting socks for the hospital….
I have to continue to exhibit "Grey Power"—
for the next generation of women
who are as sick

of these goddamned
sentences
as I am.

A moment remembered

There is a kind of beautiful mist in the morning
When you are on the water
That you view with a kind of hushed awe,
Hoping that it will last just a little longer;
And even while you watch it, and experience it, and feel,
(Just for a tiny second)
A part of it,
At the same time
You feel
you intrude,
and so, inexplicably (for you are all alone)
You hold your breath,
And barely move,
Hoping, that with a momentary cessation of movement,
You will hold onto it
Forever.
Then, you move gently into it,
and it touches your face,
in the sweetest, misty rain;
A kind of beauteous, magical, cloud,
that brings you to its breast,
And embraces you,
to express its happiness
that you took the time
to admire
something
So simple.
You feel warmed, even as you are refreshed, and wet, in the midst of this
evermoving, simaltaneously happy/sad, veil of tears—
Like an affirmation for trying,

And not so much visible, as becoming a living part, of some kind of
Mystical cycle
Of effort.

Flowers here, and…..

All friends with smiles—Ha!

Illustration 3 "Friendly Peeking"   Pen and Ink sketch   by Dawn Marie Nevills

And Flowers there;

No matter where!!!!

Section 2

Poems Written in Korea

(I stayed on "Song Doh" Beach,
on the shores of Pusan Harbour, in the
"Land of the Morning Calm".)

….on the corner, was a Karaoke house, shaped exactly like a Sphinx!!!
(smiling, of course…)

April 1997

I have looked at myself, critically,
and wondered, somewhat dispassionately
If my mind ever shows itself
In my body, in my clothes—in my outer shell.
I feel I give myself, and my continuing concern, away, at such moments;
The lengthy minutes of awkwardness, slightly unsteady hands,
screaming out silently
In a second of upset store items,
Must shout my embarassment, an apology—unintelligibly, of course—to the world.
I feel I must apologize, with my gaze,
Knowing the meant, dancing grace.
In silly, self-indulgent seconds
I imagine Stephen Hawking, and Brilliant others
Gently chiding me, with affection, for my vanity, and my sadness.
The world can only know the thoughtful silences,
The mute dreams of language barrier, the aching loving
that I offer
In shy portions, like medicinal doses
Of my medievally shy heart.

April 25, 1997

I listen carefully
When certain people are thought of
With discomfort
And disdain
For wanting
Something better.
I hear the words "unrealistic expectations",
Muse on the phrase, "Won't settle down",
Turn over the thought "Should just be glad",
And pause;
Then I look for the rope
that keeps the boat
Tied to the moorings,
Or the sinner
Tied to the mast.
And me?
I guess I'm too concerned with
Steering
To lose too much sleep, over
The rest
Of the story….

April 25, 1997

Examined and discussed Picasso's "Girl in a Mirror", today,
In my adult English Teachers' conversation class:
Every effort to see the observed
And the observing
Was made—and I, the observer of the observers,
Was, I think, also observed, mutely.
(Pity: an extra voice in the conversation would have been
Another enlightening presence....)
Every line, surely, had a deeper meaning;
Every stroke, surely, one of genius;
But, finally,
it became less art
And more science—
Like his life, surely.
Perhaps that was the struggle…
To achieve the balance he saw
In her face,
while still having to show
That inside—at least in his
List of priorities—
she was "just" an
Empty vessel.
"Oh, punctuation!"
I wonder if another man
Would have concentrated on
The beauty, and the science,
Above the shoulders?

Surely, that's a woman's
Private thanks
For
A Cameo.

May 13, 1997

The rain beats like some kind of comforting drum,
Filling my life (and my water tank on the roof) again,
As I splash home to my tiny balcony garden (in pots overlooking the sea),
Of begonias, ivy, and roses
(given later to the ladies on the waterfront to love, as I did).
I feel like some hesitant plant,
Finally freed of weeds and garbage
By some
Kind Gardener's hands.
The hot, steaming coffee pouring
inside of me
Feels like a balm,
Warming me, again, and
I swing my new fisher king's bucket
With a kind of unapologetic joy
In my unabashed tomboyishness (never quite outgrown)
Anticipating, of all things, cleaning;
Knowing my capability for ladylike behaviour,
But glorying in the capacity
to slosh through puddles, instead.
Quietly smiling inside at the children quietly smiling back at me,
and sharing our secret giggles at my
Inappropriate, unfashionable, forever practical,
(Perhaps a little plain-looking)
Canvas headwear(sort of Katherine Hepburn, in defiance, and on working holiday),
I think that today, snuggling inside my old navy cardigan,
there is a slightly wild greyness,

To the sea
That I could almost reach out and
touch…

May 24, 1997

A harbour recital in Pusan

The sea in the harbour, on this cool evening,
Is like some gently rippling dance floor of glass,
With the boats—great and small partners alive
Upon its surface—
Gliding gently across it.
Some are like awkward young lovers, hovering in one spot,
Shyly moving in hesitant circles around each other,
And slightly afraid to move too close to those other,
Gently rhythmic, majestic sea dancers—
Or perhaps they softly make way for those
On the floor
Sure of their steps, as they lead off to other
Dances, far away.
Oh, there are the clowns, too: they go
Speeding about, with brief bursts,
Their steps soon bored,
After the first rush of air past their ears;
But the others shake their knowing little flags
With exasperated affection,
their little eye lights twinkling back merrily, in the dark,
and go on,
Keeping Time.

Friday, June 6, 1997

Seaside Storytelling

Oh, when, in wondrous days, I hear
The calming waters, musically
Play, in waves, that calming song
Of happiness, and places far away
From here;
I listen not to idle, seaside chatter,
But friendly Nature's storytelling
Of travelling;
Of sadnesses on distant shores;
Of busy hands, and loneliness,
and children's hopes, which
Seem, in the listening, to be
An unbroken trill—
Not cognisant of any barriers in
Language, or perspective,
But only of joy in reaching
The listeners, and the remembered feeling of the
Comfort, and warmth, of a
Full stomach.

On Buddhists

WE are never too old, I have been told by older others, for whom I have deep respect,
To learn
From
Each other.
My bald brothers
I have learned much
From you
and your funny
Orange suits, (some with plaid fedoras, and twinkling eyes)!
You hold yourselves
So regally
In the face of so much
That should disgust
And dissuade
in these moments.
I only hope that when I remove myself
And send my thoughts into the sky
We mingle
And gather
Strength
From our shared
Beings.
I feel so different
Having made contact
With all of you.
And I, the product of so many different traditions
Steadfast in my trust in Faith
And in my Creator
While respecting yours, and That Same, who brings us closer in our love,

Can only marvel at
Your wisdom.
I can only hope to retain the
Strength
I have felt around me
When I think of
all of you.

To men angry and afraid

What is it about some men, that they would rather
Follow someone who appeals to their own frustrations
Rather than listen to a woman
Who seems a bit strange, a little eccentric, it's true—you know; a bit of an egghead…
Judy would laugh, I know, thumbing her Bible,
Being a practical United Minister—and I
an aggravated Anglican.
Why, I wonder, is there now just the shell of a building,
yet surrounded by the gentle hands of God's wider gifts?
Oh, go ahead; laugh—I do—and ridicule, too; rejoice at success
and watch, doing nothing
While children
Huddle in
My doorway, playing hopefully with hula hoops.
Is there any other place
Where they are not
Shooed away for dreaming of it, secretly?
What does it signal that what was once
Only for the Dead
Now blooms,
Changed?
To me, it speaks of that one thing that young and old alike share….
Hope.
And it is not specific to one's skin colour,
the political correctness of one's sense of
Respect,
one's economic status,
Or the place
In which

Ignorant men
Place
One.
That I am still here
And not ashamed, in the least,
Of where I live
Should be full evidence
Of my strength,
And I can still believe that flowers are still beautiful
And wild, countryside blooms
Are not made less of a gift
Because they bloom around what was once
A funeral home
or
A whorehouse…or……a guesthouse.

But—

I speak of my own country, far away, and where I live, when I am there—not here,
in this seaside place,
where salt air peppers the laundry I have hung upon the balcony dryer, again, and sunshine
softly blows it to starched dryness.

Now, both it, and I, are something else, like the result of all transformations,
and "jessie and me" just refuse
to judge a book
By its cover.

Untitled

The one that I hold very dear
Has a broken binding
And is tattered
But still warms with the inspiration of words—
Best and most precious jewel of my literary collection, blessed as I am.
Who has never
Despite
Updates
Despite
Ridicule
Despite
Battering
Despite
All these things, done and done to,
Ceased to
Inspire
Me.

Illustration 4 "Holy host"   Pen and ink sketch by   Dawn Marie. Nevills

Celebrating Singspiel's victory (of the Triple Crown) with genuine affection and good humour after watching it, on CNN

Victory, today.
Is this winning, then?
Such graceful, shared success, from thee:
Why, then, is there no surprise from me?
Perhaps (love) I expect such unexpected humility
in a realistic royal.
"Ah; it is my faith", you state, somewhat
Dryly, I think. (Yet, I detect a twinkle…joy!
You're shocked at my customary knowledge, and affectionate respect….)
It's a shame, still, that Chivas, or Passport
Had nothing to do with it. (I smile, here, briefly, stifling—successfully—

A roaring session of laughter
to which I succumb, as I type this....)
No doubt, though, that
Crown Royal is in
A simple braid, no matter where
It's placed. (You finally laugh.)
A woman, after all, has always
Had to
Carry more weight upon
Her head....

Section 3:

"A Return to Sender"

Coming Home

I remember, with some amusement, the clanking feeling of the plane's landing gear,
Which sent momentary shock waves rumbling through the passengers, when they realized
That it was temporarily stuck.
The young Jewish boy sitting beside me (I had given him the window seat)
Looked slightly panicked, and glanced sideways at me,
Searching wildly for the barf bag he knew had to be
SOMEWHERE!
I merely thought…."God, I hope he doesn't throw up all over me"…
Then I smiled at him, waited for the pilot's voice, (which seemed rather
DELAYED
If somewhat BREATHLESS IN PROTESTATIONS OF NO PROBLEMS),
And all the while, I watched the fog swirl in around us,
In a kind of daze, myself….
It seemed too dark to still be in the clouds.
Then we bashed into the runway,
and I felt Canada.
I remember having a wild thought about politics
And men
At that particular moment, grumpily,
And attempted a slight bounce.
But my gaunt, pale young companion had
Broken out into a kind of sickly recognition,
And slumped, deflated, and nauseous, in his seat.
I patted his hand, cursing quietly under my breath, feeling protective. I didn't feel well, myself.
A moment or two of lurching towards lights, (the sheen turning to a fine sweat on his face, with every fling)
and then…
The plane stalled—on the runway. I rolled my eyes, sighing,

And thought, for a moment or two, again,
Of politics.
Then the engines roared to life again, (a secret rumbling laughter, it seemed to me)
And my stomach, which had rumbled its own rather quiet—
If somewhat worried—
Signal of the fullness of its contents,
Subsided, gurgling its unhappiness.
Somewhat belatedly, I considered Gravol, encompassing.
The lights beckoned just ahead,
And the square, immaculate building
Blinked its blinkers sleepily,
Extending its cornered shape reassuringly
Through the fog.
("The pilot is probably swearing", thought I, and smiled to myself, conspiratorially.)
I wondered if he had planned a particularly Romantic evening,

(Once he had changed his briefs), and had gotten a little ahead of himself…
Or, if he was even more glad than I,
For those winking lights.

On love and hate

There is a difference, I note, presupposing in my theorizing,
Between the methods of hate and love.
Hatred always shows itself in its attempts
To use and manipulate
For its own purposes.
It is a comment which thinly disguises open racism;
A look that suggest dismissal;
A gesture that defines the essence of the
lack of respect
Which prompted it.
Love, often, is harder to actually discover:
it refuses to use the same methodology, frequently,
You see.
It relies on simpler things,
Like
Truth,
and Spirit,
discipline,
respect, admiration, encouragement, and, yes, worry—
Which is offered as mutual,
While often recognizing the lack of
its return.
Often, too, it cannot be seen,
and is frequently
Clothed in
Unexpected
Ways and
Places....

On-line farming

Within the confines of literary combines
Betwixt and between
Whether fat or lean
The expression of expression
Travels….

Musical accompaniment

The harmony achieved by concerted effort
Is more than a team sport;
It's orchestrated talent, in motion,
Of emotion.

Toronto Arrival

There seemed to be so many people,
And I hung back,
Acutely aware of my reduced weight,
And my hat.
I thought that the escalator would never end,
But I wasn't sure that I wanted it to.
For a wild moment I dreamt that
it had changed direction,
Sorry for its error,
And I was gliding back to an apology,
But the droning hum of the iron stairs continued, and so did I.
I stepped off at the bottom, sighing,
Feeling like an alien being, in my own country.
Speakers barked out flight announcements,
I silently remarked on the screaming cleanliness of the place,
Bodies milled about, cooing and harumphing their welcomes,
and clasped each other, laughing.
The Jewish boy was enveloped into his large mother,
and nearly collapsed in thankfulness, anticipating culinary predictability, and non-shifting, non-lurching, ground. "Oh Canada"….
I just felt…….odd.
Detachedly, I watched a carousel, as bags began to move
into the space,
And in a kind of floating moment of fatigue
I saw a young man, slightly sunburned, in a white shirt,
the earring giving him a slightly rakish look,
Smiling at me.
It was a full fifteen seconds—a terribly long fifteen seconds—
Until I recognized
My husband.

The word seemed harsh in my mind, a misuse, uncomfortable, and awkward,
Like a mouthful of something not quite familiar;
Not quite THERE…
And I smiled back, calmly, accepting the small bouquet,
Exchanging grim kisses,
Feeling a flood of feeling in my privates
which signalled the possibility of imminent sex,
And feeling….
Overwhelmingly, unbearably, unendurably
Shy.
The kind of man/husband/being and I
Walked around each other,
Not quite touching,
Terrified, sad/happy/gladly/sadly/apologetically exchanging words,
And began to
Move
Very
Fast.
He paced around the carousel, gazing for each bag,
Whirling it onto the cart in a kind of
Panicked haze, reminiscent of all the shouting telephone calls overseas,
And manically manoevered it
into a parking garage,
Only to discover that
There was
No entrance
To the
Correct area…
And…
We ended up back at the carousel—naturally.
I noticed then that he had broken into a fine sweat—
A kind of light sheen, that made his face glow—and he wiped at it, before

Driving the cart into a wall.
At that point
I quietly suggested that he get the car,
And I walked very sedately, and silently, pushing the cart ahead of me,
As he
Loped out of the building,
Nearly colliding
With
Four taxis.
It was four, not one, because he began to weave wildly around the first one,
Not seeing the second one,
And while swearing at the second one, upon recognition of its presence,
He did not see, with his head turned, the third and fourth, inching along
To find a parking space
in front of
The building, until…
They honked.
I laughed, then, very, very, loudly—actually stopped,
As I carefully slid the bags off of the cart,
And guffawed a kind of roaring, unladylike, harsh, bitter, bellowing, howl
Of space-filling hahahahahahaha,s, which echoed about, bouncing off of each other,
And careening into the ears of suddenly-very-awake, momentarily—arrested, passersby,
As I looked around, straightening my hat,
And searching for the (I had hoped everyone would think)
Other shocking person who had erupted like that
into

Solid, screamingly inappropriate
Laughter.
Suddenly, my smile
Turned into a more appropriate

Instantaneously, punch-in-the-kidneys
Gut-searing pain flash of
Twelve years.
I slept then—for several weeks, I think—gladly.

The secret sock (a joke with the Pope)

My cerebral cortex
is connected to my hands
Causing "I think; therefore I am" to make sense, after all:
Philosophical meanderings on the state of being
involves
Concrete thought, and, in that, there is substance:
Wonder what the old Soc would think of that one?
Probably just lean on his, and yawn, impatiently, a rather unphilosophical
Twinkle in his eyes…
Caned comfort, winkered.
I still feel the bruises.

The Weather's fine

Merry is as merry does
And merry meant is as merry wuz
Being constant with the fuzz, and all that…
So, being naughty, in a dotty
Kind of way
makes your day (or so you say).
Come on inside…and play!
Aw….feeling a bit "under the weather" today?
Methinks it could be a musical ride!

Building Blocks

The controversy
Of poverty
Covertly
Covering
Nothing
Mocks
The glut
of bricks
Available for
Masons everywhere…
Neatly placed,
Each in their space,
We trace
A pattern
Of growth,
Like some huge
Chart of
Mission: Erase Destitution.
Each contribution, then,
Makes restitution, Friend;
This is YOUR case;
Make it happen:
Humanity, Humility, and Habitat
Announce their connections,
And we, each of us,

Must learn
To
B.uild **A.**gain
and
M.ake **D.**o.

Wednesday, July 22, 1998

Morning Puffs (looking at the stacks, watchfully, while working at Esso)

Gleaming silver, grey and black;
Huge metaphysical totems to our
Technical ability to feed from
Mother Earth,
that we may crawl, snail-like,
Upon Her surface.

Saturday, August 01, 1998

More-Musical Accompaniment

In this sometimes mad race to be the most enabled
it is often humbling
To perceive
that
The simplest instruments
The simplest words
the simplest
Often
Teach us the most.
Whether we listen or not
is often dependent upon our ability
to separate the caucophony
From the
Symphony.
What was it they said, long ago, about white noise?
Perhaps I, like many,
Missed the
Point.
There must have been too many for
My simple mind
To
Understand.

Descriptive sign at war memorial

Guts-smeared-in-teary-eyed memory windshield mess…
Sister site in montana/british columbia area. (head smashed in buffalo jump)

My poems: for me, they spell "the rap...y?" *(Scene:Ipperwash/Azhoodena)*

A)

Talk, talk, talk…

Talk, talk, talk…

Talk, talk, talk…

"Oh, where is the chalk? I need to see an outline first. What is the purpose of this lesson"?

(I can't hear you…)

"Do you know sign language?"

(This means stop, please. Why do I hear, "gogogo?"…..pardon?)

B)

(Writer's note: look for metaphorical imagery and sound relation, rather than literal, literary translation. Speech pattern sounds, stuttering, modes of communication, sociological ramifications, the place of women in society, and how all of these, encompassed, (sometimes in a hug) might be

interpreted, and "**why**"…always, I end up asking the same question.)

C)

Driving-heads-hanging-out-guts-abdomen—blood-wet-tears-agony,…no translation available, as of yet. (heart)

The trouble with tracing

Has been rectified.

Be
Low (a brief haiku)

Urp.

Living near water

Take me to the seaside, so I can watch the waves
Kiss the shore, glad to reach it, at last.
That gentle meeting is the greatest sight,
Like two old lovers, embracing night, and each other,
As the moon sets the pace,
And the stars stand on guard, silently approving,
The sky, a huge velvet blanket for the moving
Forces beneath it.

Runway Romance (a late birthday gift)

I met you on the way to somewhere;
Suddenly my destination could wait,
And the boarding call sounded like some muffled echo
in the recesses of my pounding heart.
For just a brief second, recognition
Clanged its
Arrival,
And glimmering eyes
Meant something more than just
A ticket to
Freedom,
As we clasped hands,
and you raised mine
To your lips,
As if it was some loved wine
you had thirsted for, these years gone;
And I? I learned what it was to
Wait at the station…..
In my mind, it is all I can do, to give you
The rose.
It says volumes—and I can't, as usual.
I see you keep it in a safe place, these days…dapper and smart as ever, with some depth, rediscovered.
Makes me think of poetry,
And your bearing, when I close my eyes, reminds me of
Some great, strong Pine.
And you? You are the song of songs, within my compass set, and each time I imagine us, as we were,
We are young again.

Penny Lover

I must admit to being a great respecter
Of the penny.
Rolled up together,
They send such smiles
To those outstretched hands
Whose connection to dreams
is often only a prayer to Heaven
For receipt of Them.

Syntactical Discourse

Not being one to
Digress, overmuch;
Perchance, an examination of the superfluous
Might reveal
Ubiquitious profundity,
Excelling…
"Shite", slangly speaking.

Time passes

I look back on my life, thus far, and
Realize, as do others,
How choices we make
Affect our
Gravity.
NOT seriousness, you understand:
My attempts at humour have always been somewhat
Er**, original**, if sometimes morbid, riDICulously complex—and my spelling often leaves something to be
desired….
Nevertheless, small achievements, less grandiose, less important, (perhaps to the world—but not in a J.A. sense),
Are so very fleeting;
But sometimes
Deeper, more pained, and grieving, really, than first observed, upon closer scrutiny:
And I, quietly celebrating the first glimpse of a cucumber, in the midst of my tears.

I have a kind of spatial mind

I have a kind of spatial mind, susceptible to those unkind
Words, which,
Dartlike, leave little dents on the surface of my heart,
Which often jumps in front,
To shield my
Cerebellum.
I suppose we are all motivated by different stimulii,
But most think on the level, don't they?
Otherwise, what good is a healthy brain massage?
If something else pops up,
Who am I to argue with
Forward-thinking…..?
It's all in the delivery, right?
Sighs aren't quite compleat without the
"L", and so with skirts….ALAS!

The moon is full, this civic day, and I must travel

I just love the innocent things—
Like falling in love, and fresh cut chippies,
And moonlight on the water.
Now, if only there was live jazz,
I might have stayed for a while—but I feel from a lost era.
That's one thing I really miss
About S(e)oul…
Even in the midst of all those people with whom I could not speak,
I never felt
Alone.

Illustration 5 "Sing gai jing!" Self portrait, Pen and ink sketch by Dawn Marie Nevills

<u>Sing, gai jing!</u>

Sing, gai jing, though words are strange;
We hear the love—and it's the same….

<u>In praise of jazz</u>

Give me a bit of Miles, to take along the road
Of life,
I'll travel on and listen to the same thing—genius in composition.
(At least on a good, clear day…)
And, if it's not fusion within the constructs of harmony
It'll get me there, just the same.
Perhaps, as I turn the corner of life, a little Nina Simone will creep in
With deep tones, and throaty versions of life's little laneways;
Later, I'll reminisce about other trips, where I mused on the loss of women
Like Billie Holliday, taken too soon, for something stupid;
And then I'll turn to Miles, again, with little Junior Waler thrown in, for
Good measure (one must remember one's roots, after all…)
This little recipe of life contains many flavours in your ear, after all; brand new,
And T-bone, too…
But how tangled can the skeins become?
Jazz makes 'em, and jazz breaks 'em,
and then just gently overtakes them,
(never mind the power of the tune…)
It's the real notes that matter, in the matter, I am told…(I laugh.)
There's always Steely Dan, and The Strawbs, to fall back on, if you need the rest
Of the best—
Or just a little pitter patter in the fog of the mix.
(Memo to myself: Be nice, be real, be fine
And you might know a Valentine….
Or—Better still—a happy face stamp, in place of mine.)

A poem about racism

When you looked at my face, today
What did you see?
I say "what", because you could not have seen
A person.
If you had seen a person
You would have spoken
If you had seen a person
You would have spoken to me, not shouted around me.
If you had seen a person
You would have seen
My eyes.
You would have known that I care for you,
Though you may not have cared for me.
Tell me now, Friend;
Do we understand each other
any better, now that we have both
Lost face?

Small tears

I don't know if you can see the importance of a smile
Where before there was a frown.
Perhaps it's not important to
Big men with
Bigger machines
That little smiles
Do not happen, as a result
Of ALL big decisions:
Rather, sometimes only small attempts, joined.
Perhaps small tears justify the ridiculousness of
The fires that they
Put out—
But they are still small victories, amidst the grime, and the sadness, and the heat.

These grey days

These grey days, (as we grow greyer, and more aware of life, in all its forms)
Life presents itself as a kind of symphony of understanding…in shades that remind one of history,
And manners.
Perhaps a throwback to banking days are too subtle, suggestively speaking,
But I believe in a kind of blending of
Intellectual peripherals,
And artistry of formulae is not lost, on those who
Dwell more on
Literary matter.
Both are the result of the
Creative spark, the fine blooming of an idea,
Still unexplained,
(And not necessarily
Required, at that;)
This seeing with greater depth,
Which is the result, not of experimentation, but, ultimately,
Of thoughtful silence, and has to be enough, at last.
Like humility,
The ego, enjoying
Respite from its
Own pursuits,
is Quieted, somewhat forcibly, and suddenly very aware of its place
in the tapestry of
Life.
There is a place for ego, after all…how silent it is, without song.

My Friend Jennie

Left a message of hope for my friend Jennie, today;
it wasn't anything like a note—
Just a postcard
In a gypsy herb basket;
A picture of a sailing ship,
and a list of the Rotary Club's four principles,
As a reminder of how important
Her presence was
In that place, despite her depression.
And, as I left, I saw the two chairs, like old friends, carefully placed
On either side of the old, antique, desk—one for her, one for me—
and thought of the importance of
Old Girls, helping each other—and a little Spencer….(smile.)
What is the good of pottery, after all,
If you can't share it?

Dancing for Ribbons

Saw the single horses, head and shoulders high,
Trotting with defiance, noses to the sky;
The ribbons in their manes, proudly saying to the crowd
They need carry no cruel rider, shouting long and hard;
And, as each bucked the discipline, that made him stand so still,
Each prancing heart did dance with joy, at the unseen Captain, on the hill.

At the Carnival

What does it take to put the joy back into the carnival?
Giving a few tickets to a little boy, so he can ride on the ferris wheel with his father?
Spotting a big boy a buck or two so he can get a little necklace with his name on it,
Since he is proud of it, now? (And where was HIS father, again, today?)
Doing a little jig, just for sport, and smile, egging them, successfully, to turn the music back on?
Smiling and laughing, which is always infectious?
Posting a little sign, so the carnival people can see it, when they walk tiredly down the street seasonally
flush, and enjoying their brief breaks?
Or does it simply take
A little whistling?
A walk through the carnival makes you feel a child again,
For a few moments.
An older brother learns to care for his little brother,
And good feelings
Fly, like
Jets of fine hearts
in a sky
Crowned with
Whispers of clouds.
And I?
I remember being at the
Wheel, again,
And how a man/boy, for a few moments, can experience the unique therapy
That is
The Carnival.

No one can ever replace that cold, crisp day,
Caramel apple's juice dripping down my chin,
Laughter in my heart, sunshine dancing merrily off of the lions and the tiger and the bears (oh, my!),
Magic in my hands,
Smiles in my mind,
speeding on the Zipper of
My life.
These days, I just stand a little more silently,
Encouraging….
And hope that every child, (young and old)
Gets a chance to go, and,
For a few short hours,
Be Young, and Free, again.

My canine companion

I remember going to the Humane Society, that day, long ago.

I had gone in search of a little dog, a quiet dog, a Yorkie, perhaps;

A dog which required

A tired, less spirited companion.

A dog which required less love, possibly.

A dog which did not suffer the results of

Unkind hands, while looking for

Healing ones.

Silly me…

As usual, I ended up with

Something else, entirely.

I ended up with

A dog with

A temporary bladder problem (which she presented to me, at the Humane Society, apologetically, mortified, and obviously having been beaten for it

—later I discovered that someone had bashed her over the back with a two-by-four piece of wood, and loud noises caused involuntary bladder release still,—this, in a puppy…She had been around guns, too. Potty training took us six months and a lot of spread out green garbage bags in the spare room, along with sudden runs down the stairs to the parking lot.)

A fear of people

A fear of storms, (and their associated memories, possibly, not being able to ask)

A dog in shock.

Of course, I took her home

To carry her down from the second flight

Twice daily, in order to urinate on

My attempts at a garden, in the midst of a gravel parking lot.

(I grew squash, which covered the entire area, in protest, when the landlord threatened to pave it,
but, giving in with an exasperated, but affectionate, sigh, he ended up leaving me a lovely border area of flowers and neat vegetable rows, swearing slightly)

The other times, she lay in the corner, not moving,

While people said to me

"That dog, when she wakes up, will kill someone.

If I were you, I would shoot it, or leave it to be

Put down."

I would scowl dangerously....

(Part 2 — Return from Comatose — "The Brandy Bark")

One day, instead of remaining oblivious to the world,
She got up from the corner, actually looked at me, and lay down, sighing, at my feet.
Later that afternoon, she trotted down the stairs
and scratched at the door, hopefully…
Barking, for the first time in our friendship.
(Tears actually came to my eyes.)
(Of course, this progressed into a rather overprotective "hurling herself at the door", when someone
knocked upon it, but we continued to strive for, ah, **balance**…and it was the return of the "three a.m. shouter", drunk again, and
Unable to accept that no one he knew lived there, anymore, anyway, that made me grateful she was there—though concerned that she might hurt herself, flying against the steel, like that, protectively…
I was always rather glad of the steel mesh over the window portion, then—but appreciated the "hurling", even more.
I often wondered if he was the one that had been phoning and terrifying me, too…)
That eruption of bark noise was the sweetest of music
To my ears, (which I played to her, as she lay in the corner…)and
I can remember talking to my parents about that afternoon,
and seeing both of them, in my mind's eye,
Shaking their heads with affectionate, mild, exasperation;
Mindful of the little girl
Who brought home all sorts of strays, human and animal,
And smiling, sadly.

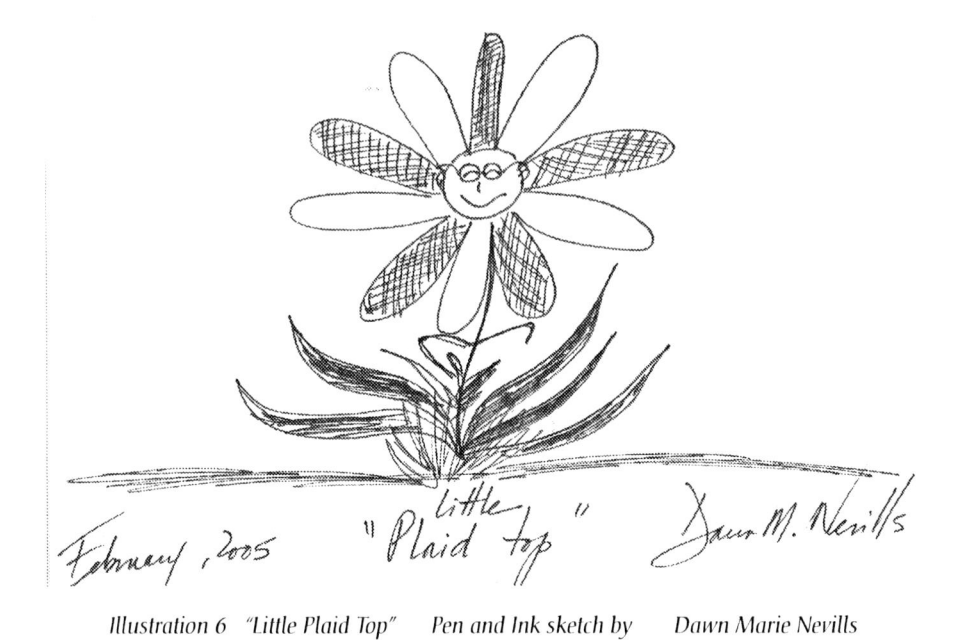

Illustration 6   "Little Plaid Top"   Pen and Ink sketch by   Dawn Marie Nevills

Section 4:

The Brothers Grimm

The untouchables

We are the untouchables.
We have watched, grieving, while what used to be a proud tradition
is turned into a club
Where only those
Who treat the job
As a joke, (while collecting, on the side,
the fruits of their deceit),
Get good press.
The rest get manoevered—
Through politics,
death threats,
mortgage loss,
and loss of peer ego—
Into pulling the trigger
Of today's latest "hasty pudding policy".
They are never to be found, these fleeting shadows,
When the tears,
On both sides,
Begin.
We have made "us"
A mockery of what every child
Used to want to be.
WE beat ourselves, each other, and the world—
With our platitudes, our removed sense of justice, and
Our hypocritical implementation of
Policies
which we have created, hurriedly,
For our own protection,
While throwing them, like so many pieces of brushwood,
(Those sensitive, knowing souls on both sides,)

On the fire of our
Egos.
Then we stand back, contemplatively,
And analyze
How they burn.
No wonder they walk, gloved hands in time,
In grim recognition
Of
another offering
Thrown to the
Snow wolves.

Sometimes

Sometimes, after hours and hours of thinking, I must quietly speak;
Not lightly, but with light.
Not in vain, but for that vein of good that still must exist.
If it has merely gone to sleep for a while,
I will awaken it, and smile at its blossoming,
for the gentle reminder of Young that will always be
in a few of us
Shall never die…
We shall "make it sew".

Everything old is new again…an ode to recycling

Just think; if freeroute maps could be sewn into quilt patterns,
What should we be able to do?
Gardens with aerial signals; place settings with priorities:
The possibilities are endless, really.
It's the little things that accomplish some really wonderful
Examples of communication.
Even fashion has its own diction, and membership, even when secondhand…
Just watch the best of what we loved in history resurfacing in our outer shells
(Heart of gold, and all that…),
Catwalk and canvas can do miracles.
You'd be surprised to know who still cares, deeply, creative hearts, all,
and who is glad to know them, seeing that good beyond the paint;
Knowing that there is"art with heart" in even the strangest places!

Burdens

These hours of sleepless, numbing, watching, with an ear to history,
the examples of war-shocked, despairing inabilities to communicate,
Reach deep into me, into my being, wounding;
and, feeling a small part of the pain, I cannot stand idly by,
Careless and uncaring,
Within this pulsing family of
Humanity.

Section 5:

Love Poems

Untitled

Somehow, this day cannot just pass,
Hours and minutes ticking away, like some tortuous metronome.
I would demand that you arrive in front of me, momentarily,
If it weren't so laughable.
I would stamp my foot, even! (washed earlier, twinkling just) churlishly,
determinedly—still shorter than
you,
Glaring defiantly at you—a silent order—your eyeballs rolling heavenward, with
humour, but mine—
the glint still there, flashing.
"No excuses", since you have declared this day
My victory.
Fly to me, low-throated rumbling,
that stirs my trembling limbs like
some instant thrill of fire
In my heart…I would reach for you,
Covering you, like cummings' sky.

About socks

Socks…
Wonderful guts of sheep
That give me shivers of the service I deserve
When I demand it.
Me, the modern woman
Who admits to being alive.
Who shames no one with her acknowledgement of having
A brain
As well as breasts.
Socks…
Wonderful control of my own body
Wonderful celebration of shared passion
Between a man and wife
Socks…
Wonderful gentleman's example
Of mutual submission
to maturity,
no frustration
and responsibility—
FACE TO FACE.

<u>Gaze glazing</u>

This evening, as I walked along the quiet country road, gentle cover of snow
Melding Season's touch with earth and such,
A glow
Upon it, sheen-like, blinking back at me with sky pure gleam,
Newly dropped,
Stunned me into warmth of gazing;
And in that still moment of seconds suspended, hanging there, like
Ticking metronomal orchestration,
The flakes swayed, and swayed,
Their tick-tick jest of never ceasing movement, gentled,
and, landing still, tumbled into one another, joining, finally, into one
Huge, layered, ice cake blanket.
Silenced thus, by twining lace of frothy covering, spread
Out like liquid Northern Comfort upon hard surface sleeping,
I stood, and drank, breathing repletedly, then closed my eyes,
and slipped beneath, sighing signal recognition
that you were there, on fire, beneath the ice, like me, and dancing in the sky—a
mirror of our joy.
The stars blinked back, humming and twinkling their shared secret,
Approvingly,
As two bodies tumbled and clung together in the suddenness of the
Lake of their dreams, prehistorically perfect.

Explained depths

I am thy comfort, thee would say:
And what are thee, to me?
Thou art my air, my sky, my earth, my culinary sustenance;
My alarm, my blanket, my hands,
My water, quenching even, a thirst that never abates—
Yay, that cannot even, that WILL not, despite my yearnings against it.
Thou art my morning, understood, when pale sun lights a sky
That begins a new day.
Thou art my stars, my moon—pale, inadequate reflections
Of a feeling that exceeds even these
Boundaries of time and space;
Thou art a madness, a healing, a hidden, encompassing feeling,
Powered, powerful, empowering:
My bodily blood—that long-ago symbol, coursing through me
With the life, the enormity, the shock of its totality,
Beyond even thy own
Comprehension;
The underestimation of quiet capacity, a usual, and noted, thing.
Perhaps—or perhaps not (I shudder, pondering it)it is
Reflected in thy burning ice eyes, silently, gently, flickering, and we finally
See each other.
I think I am dying, and yet I see you walk, and live.

Portrait of a filled sweater

Six foot, thee,
Nor dic, Fan to sea…
Wot, you are!
Silvered foxy (kissing doc C)
—with a proxy—
But you…bizqwik—a door!
See it open, like a flower
Petalled, vibrant passion bower
Warmth, and heat and gentle touch
Leads to longer, deeper words and much
Smores. (My gentle discipline, smiling, quick flick on lips, yours now, silent.
Wah!)

34, and I implore
my Penn to stop—
it won't…and on, anon,
Another "little death",
Welldone!

A whale of a thought…

Oh dear, I have a headache, which I have given myself, with too much worrying, again.

I think that it might explode.

Wouldn't it be strange, all of these tears suddenly gushing in a geiser

Out of the top of my head?

(Mayhap I'll be a fountain, watering my garden—

a goodly thing to do with one's life.)

My secret burdened one, I sent you a part of it, that day,

A surprising, stolen moment of not quite giving myself away…

Perhaps a little, clerically.

Did you feel me, peeking out from amongst those blooms on page?

My disappearing grin, leaving you wondering for just a second, out of your busy agenda;

Ah…you've found me out, after all—and me so careful with the postmark!

(I grin)

A poem here

Like an arrow, straight and narrow, I fly
To your heart
(it being half
Of mine.)
Joined thusly, thinking, all the while,
Of organs, surgery, and such things
Like as not, I should celebrate this
Metaphysical travelling,
Yet despair at its still innate
Unconscious, inadequate
Connection.
Oh, heart of my heart, my other part,
Close your eyes, dream that these delicate touchings
Are yet on your face,
And thine, on mine.
Then, this rude thing, in its joining,
Might yet reach
Another plane,
And we two,
On it, gliding,
Looking down, even, on that
"Bridge Across Forever"
Je t'adore, completez,
Quietly.

<u>A poem there</u>

I exist in your eyes
And when you look at someone
You share my heart
In your response to
their troubles.
Only think of me, your heart, your eyes, waiting, hugging you warmly
and know that somehow, we two
Will assist
In these ever-present efforts
When you try,
Difficult as it is for us
To touch
Across this time and space
Of years and responsibility
To plain and bliss, where we exist, somehow, in each other's minds.

Sandbox silliness

Moo cow eyes
Mud pies
Better shiver
With those slivers of
Quiver,
Winking lights….!

….for if i thought, even for just a moment,
that your hot hand upon my breast
could cool a season,
i would fling myself in the snow,
and beg you to cover me,
tumbling, steaming—
though alive only to you,—seeing through these tears, at last.
only stop, then, wildly, i beg you,
and see, first, what fires burn
in my eyes—my
silent
command,
your fall
to
grace;
to ecstasy.
Oh, God! If only I were different, and did not love, so…!
despite your mumbled prayers;
then I could sleep, not thinking of you.
Damn, my goodness!
I would burn in the snow, naked, instead, with you,—but, may
God forgive me,
I would be at peace. Oh, for that hand, never mocking me! How it
 would love my aching heart.
Instead:close round firm, each controlled stroke—lest I die!..

go on; lift, then.
i should like to see your smile, as i
raise myself upon
this steel
pole
again—

just don't forget to
breathe.
now stare, again, stare!
just say nothing—
there is no conscience in this fire of my making: ice is what you'll
 forget.

we shall see—tiger or tamer?—
who is the whip, and if it's me.
I doubt there will be much "speaking."
you, (as always), will be much too concentrated. (You put a finger to
 my lips when I say "focused", ever pacifist. So sweet!)
i shall "focus" on task at hand, then….two more crunches, please!
 (You laugh, so quietly, to yourself, reading, cereal urge…)you'll
 see i'm not winking. the stare is….connection, no matter how
 brief.
i am just quieter, and much more deliciously dangerous, apres
 grief:(how i mock myself!) a defiance about me,
in response to so much death. i require only this knowledge, from
 you, nothing else: that you see it.
i am much, much wilder; you see, now i am older, and care less—no;
 care more. But, you know that…

I need to be alive again—and you; you my silent, cloth-dark-metal
 sweetness, shall awaken me: did you know?Ha!
….quiet rumble, that is your sigh against my ear—and you, so
 serious, alway,
in the midst of all that is wild, and chill—"I only feel you", you say,
 "every second"….(ah, the seconds tick away)…
the soft nuzzle in my hair, that is promise and torture for you—
and all these clothes
that bar my burning;

mere layers of weight that will be shed
at last,
no matter where it is, bodily (you look at me, finally, with rolling eyes…."anywhere—just NOW")
(WE ARE EVERYWHERE, MY LIGHTENING STRIKE…)
still, silent—ah yes!slight trailing-touch-on-cheek-lightening-tremulous-in-small-shock-wave-me! **oh!…**
inside, groaning. **Oh**!…only kiss my eyes, just here, at the corner;

"**Tell me**!" you say, demanding it of me, yet so softly, searching my face, earnestly—always so worried—
(ah! gladness!) that i-feel-you-feel-me-feel-us…..strongly:
close your eyes, now—just a twinge, flutter of wings—you shall know! A small, small sigh…those eyes still make me go.
I see them everywhere, blinded as I am, by this heat.

I dreamt of you last night.
Your head was nestled against my shoulder, face to my neck, softly speaking,
And all the while, until I suddenly woke,
With a gentle shudder, (sly slight of hand)
I thought of you, until
Suddenly you were there, earnestly, against me.
I closed my eyes, sighing, and thought…"such a slick good morning", as you held my hips,
Surprised, and, laughing softly, as I tumbled over you, and rode, with a shake—
Thinking all the while—"Ah! Awake!
It's madness—herself! How sane!"(Cheeky, cheeky me….)

It seems we must give up comfortable
For savage necessity

My darling
Forgive my weakness….
Only tell me that you need me
And I will forgive myself the rest, growling.

Exquisite sentinel, drooling,
drooling….know this;
I'd make you sPeak.

of all the things i have not told you, this may be one: when i awake,
 you are my star

Two sets of fifty, sitting up, and breathing all the way;
I separated them to let the dog out—pausing just to say
Dammit.
Another twenty minutes, spent dreaming on the bike,
And then I added two kilometres, and took a quiet hike,
Thinking.
Finally, twenty back leg thrusts—you know old stubborn "donkey"
 me,
And finished; twenty pelvic thrusts—thinking only, sweet, of theee…
Loving.

Section 6:

Bean talkin' to) the impossible One"

Because of Rowin A. (addered up)

The thin blue line is a kind of Family spaghetti tradition
Which winds around various plates, like a kind of
Odd cord, which, although being edible,
is not pants.
(Well, it could be, I guess, in a strange, tectonic joebee function,
Being connected to various dinosaurs, and such, subtle undercurrents
notwithstanding,
Praise God)
I tend to shy away from those boutiques, HOWEVER, I
(whilst clearing my throat, formally, and sucking in my cheeks,
lest I give myself away, in the midst of narrowing my eyes, in another attempt to make
the newest buzby spew milk through his nose, barking uproariously—
or, even more helpful, pee his pants, laughing,—HARD—
the dark stain marking him as part of the "blackNESS", initiated and territoried,
Another "handful" being successfully completed; and I draw my little claws back in, back into
The velvet gloves of a different life, having tickled and succeeded, but still enjoying the odd
Challenge, occasionally)
Am aware of various helpful things within them,
and the spaghetti, winking its winky eye, (dewy-eyed monstering)
is quite naughty there.
However, because of rowin, and how excellent one looks, in a suit,
Pasta outdoes itself,
While Ma More is still simply the best, pennying in his door,
Smiling, old-School, that very dangerous smile of hers
(not wanting to tear the roof off of the place, just yet…but immensely enjoying
the Experience
of

Shaking the Foundations and leaving them…
…Tired.)

<u>Petals aglow woo</u>

Bubba, my bubba, I think I'll dub ya—
Not because you're uniformed,
Or Kharki and intact.
Because you are my own C.hief S.weet, Angeliculled, and calmed, by
A purring, slightly slighted, rather dangerous, true floral
Fact.
Encouraging behaving…
Moretime, methinks—
Roused, and somewhat annoyed.
Luckily, though, still fired by your face,
Despite being in it.
(Look! Look! A plane! A plane! no…a dragonfly—or maybe a
lace-covered pea, whirling—the deli being slow…)
…ah, but No! ONly me, grinning wickedly…naked, but for the hat—
Your girl from e.e.'s poem, giggling—eyes watering with mirth.
Dignified, indignant, feigning clothes, and daring you to say a word. (an odd,
rather
Duke O'Bore moment, really…)
Thinking of planes, your three—stone weight; dear me! and things party-arty.
Bucket in hand, walking sedately to meet you,
And all the while…clothed! (I smile.)
You wish to spank me, you say?
Up with those hands!
You sigh, roaring…"impossible, still"—holding them high for inspection.

<u>Wonkbonkered thusly (Farmerknighted)</u>

Willy wally wonkya
Billy bally bonkya
Tonka
Enya inya.
Dillyin'!

(Dedicated to Colin Pickles.)

Banilla

Nuts over pure screaming
Pomes glace, accented.

Style rhymes timed protection

Ticklin', taps tappin' "g" tapped, tweaze teasin'
Slip slidin', sneezin'
(Caught a cold one, am ice powered vicious for iced and innocent)
Vickered Vick, another caged and bound one, blackened all over.
B.ully, wooly, S.cully,
(so, so bold!) smile (modern sonnet)
Ooooo weeeeeeeeeeeeeeeeee!
SSSSSSSSSSSSSSSSSSSooo
FrEEEEEEEEEEEEEEEEEEeeeeeeeeeeeeeeeeeee!
(Could be.)
CCCCCCCold NO coulddue.
Man;do
Can do! BE!
Lindymyelitpsycsicm
Done, kickin'!
Personality capability, in a word
Up!

In………………crisp. Hurhuzzah! Polite, first,
Yo moma!
Worde olde.
Best'. (slighted knot belonging dyslexia) man's face next, and
Spearedaddfacenumbfeelsteel elsaclench'portantspace'tween.One.AH!
What a classical gas, dark side unfurled
Unspoken, quietly.
Slightly scary for the braveless…I smile, honoured.

On Buddha and Mountaintops

I am reminded of that tune
that speaks of God as Jah, in each man, with a wife, and child,
Alive and speaking on a mountaintop wild
Hippie-like, rather, and celebrating birthdays,
Glad to be with each other
Knowing, somehow, that I am there,
and laughing, too, with big hugs all 'round—
Although I avoid the skiing, being in
Friendship with trees, and
Having collided into one, apologizing profusely,
Last trip. (Must have been confused about the leaf aspect…)
(So much for the graceful glide!….)
See Jane skate!
V….word!
Here is my head popping up…with a smile.
Just a little elf in the snow…
Little mousie in gloves and a parka…roaring—
Con-canning.

<u>Diagram of above poem</u>

Feet

Other parts

Hands (fingers in peace sign, except for one, held up as result of undignified landing into tree and
snow)

Head (standing on it, actually)

(political/security analysis welcome—possibly foundational)

A shock of progress

And on, beneath the gazes which
yet hide amongst shadows and years,
Mere wisps of smiles remembered and unseen
throughout innocent corridors, sunny fields,
Quiet, personal library corners, those "angels of our better nature" dancing
Still, in
Festivals of affection and musical merriment—
And wry, quirking brows—
the poet plods, pilgrim-like in his search
For Himself,
Never stopping, at any point, to consider
That he had met Him
All along the way…and loved him, FOR
Himself.

The Fellowship (A merry vessel)

These good knights of our imaginings,
Whose hearts, in spite of all that is corrupt,
And rotting, and cynical beyond even the boundaries
Of their own excesses,
Are yet touched, and moved, by the quiet hand,
the juice of a newly-picked berry,
the smile, and twinkling eyes, and
Merry laughter
Of a loving heart, knowing these same as
Treasures beyond all that could, and are,
Bought and sold, of themselves—
Beyond Conscience, and Thought, and Love, in this life,
Cheap mockeries of
the Table, and the Shared Cup.

Our daily trek

My dog and I set out walking to listen to the countryside.
Sometimes, in the very early morning, small wisps of fog, left behind by early-rising angels
Who kiss the plants awake,
Linger yet awhile,
And we tread very softly, then, because I am always afraid I might disturb
One
In the midst of flight.
I think they must converse with the fairies, then, too,
As they rest their tired selves, yet awhile,
and the fairies must lament that so many don't believe in them, either—
A shared comfort between winged creatures, who guard children's hearts and happiness.
And yet Brandy and I always try to be oh, so, quiet in those special moments,
when stillness reigns, and I feel a certain gentle sigh on the wind;
For when the dew glistens like diamonds dropped by God on to the bright green blades of grass,
There seems a kind of hum, apart from crickets' busy songs, and, if I listen carefully,
I can almost, but not quite, make out their tiny voices,
Excitedly exclaiming with joy,
As I bend on knee to pick up
another discarded
Tin or bottle.
And then, oh then!…
I feel a girl again!

<u>In praise of my hero, Shakespeare (simple elogy) (…whilst enthroned)</u>

When, in times of sad restraint, my Quill does rise and shake
itself upon yon waiting page (that now is NOT so quiet and dour),
My mind—(awake amidst the sleeping crowd)—
Does stir, and then—oh then!—my eyes, (quite misted) do
Behold
Sweet words, that flow like lines of laughing gold
Upon the waiting page.
What?! Two pages? One is merry, one is wary
(Lest the steady flow, in its restraint, become too Merry)
As the words, in their great comfort, succor, (in their way),
A mind alight with words of Play.
As fingers fly, the winged travails of (reminders of the tests
Of greater things than simple womens' tasks, which do beset
Those same with consternation) this respite of the league,
Betimes, does prove that cleanly rhymes are more to
Our like. And what of it? Who is wont to say, in such a day,
that, though to read be such a boon, such simple hands
Do shame the best!
And why (amidst such wondrous egos, the likes of which do
Strut and, cock-like, exhude with remonstrance, the lofty praise
Of those, and these, and mine, and we's) write?
Still, sprightly washing, (freely scoffing), gently doffing
Feathered plumes, which tremble with
Guided wind, and
Dryly (just), blinking under a warm and chuckling sun,
Do float, (nymph-like) and wave, moretime, like
Heavenly robed;

All the more at ease, (replete, betide) with mirth of hard, wood Com Fort.

Saturday, February 5, 2000 00:50

The Night Progresses

"Tick, tick, tick, tick…"
Steady, clock-bird round, tap-tapping minutes
Into hours, keep pace with
Mournful train's puffing, haunted moan, as it
Cuts through ink-ebony sky: near, nearer…
Nearer still….then….far away, again;
Suddenly, kind, ghostly, whistle-woman, dancing
Down its snaking, steely bars, shakes
Sleepy ice-locked ground, into rumble-mumble
threats of being too disturbed,
As it stills the souls of those whose blood was
Glue for all those gleaming lines to somewhere else—
Glue eyes, peering blindly between wood slats, snow-dirt,
and track: mouthless………screaming.

Above, orange flame-flares light a troubled sky, filled with
Clouds of discontented smoke-tears, wheeling
Across the cold, black, night-canvas.

Briefly Metaphorical Feelines

The empty page spreads itself open,
A welcoming blank;
A smiling yawn of space,
Awaiting imprint, and
Grinning its vacuous void status, while
Invisibly thirsting,
Its beckon met.

<u>My Thing is My Own</u>

thrilling thing; you throbbing bit,
I can't believe that we once said
Not us! No; we'll have none of it!
(and neither of us near a bed)
Ah, Work! Ah, Love! and both (such dread)
…..A damn Fine Fit.

Deep plain maquillage (religious meanderings)

Living in the country has affected my "priorities":
I have taken to using depilatory on my typically linear eyebrow,
rather than yanking them out, one by one, in order to define the two eyes in my face,
(Despite my rather impressive tolerance for pain)—
Although I am nervous about trying it on my legs! The daisy razors, somewhat painedly, seem quite good enough, there!
I still purchase tights, hearing in my mind my mother's warning about
Horseshoe kidneys, and catching my death.
(So much for reawakening the sexual goddess in me…difficult when it's bloody cold out there.
I suspect that those ads are invented somewhere like the Canary Islands, anyway—somewhere with no winter!
…in praise of flannel nighties—hurrah!)
However, I believe that I left the cream on a tad too long,
Which explains the burning sensation on my face, and the glowing red blotches above my
eyeballs, (very sensitive to the touch)…I imagine the result on my legs, and congratulate
myself on my good judgement.
(Then again, I didn't read the directions.)
In retrospect, I ponder the symbolism, and wonder if I
Missed something,
In my small bearded state of mind, (winking slyly)
Remembering the red-faced men in church, shouting,
And thinking to myself….ooooh!…."Direction"

P.(.oem) and (S).tructure
OWNED

Once upon a time, there was a little rhyme
That didn't.
Because of its state, which, (not rhyming great)
Made it hard—
(To consider);
Other, better lilts, boasting higher, literate stilts,
Rested upon their laurels,
Alliterating wildly.
The former
Just stayed in lines…and minds.

The welcome of the Quiet Door

The welcome of the Quiet Door says,
"How can we grieve forever, we sad, concerned souls,
When Death is but another door, beyond this,
To Life in a never ending spirit embrace of
Unknown Joy?"
"Would, that after our tears have been shed,
We could, (for just a tiny second, softly), feel even a small part of such happiness,
in that state of
Being,
For those we love, and have loved,
And celebrate, in the midst of our weeping,
At their meeting together in that Place,
Where Feet are tired, rested, and bathed."

Inside

Inside my head I have often wondered if there are a series of projects
As yet unrealized.
But, in the thinking, voiced, they…happen!
It is a kind of effort/celebration of cerebral connection to my "able" self,
Shared, and created…So many things for my hands!
That must be what fills my head…
Beautiful kindness art, of the possible.

October, 2003

I was a kind of Naval dog;
They put me in the Yard;
I tried to be a "dick" while there—
(But it was very hard!)
I sate beneath a leafy tree,
Imagining life, spent—
but somehow, I confused myself!
(Not knowing what I meant)....

SNAPSHOT — Wooden Sentinel

He stood outside the hospital, leaning awkwardly—apologetically—against the weathered brick of the emerg entrance outside wall, a "disinterested blowfish" cardboard cutout of himself, puffing absently as a cigarette (which he habitually chain-smoked, like he did everything), dangling awkwardly from a leather grasp. The eyes—mild, blinking orbs, with skin stretched tight across a gaunt bulge of gelatinous suggestion—were like two wounded pits, from which two small hills jutted, suddenly. The landscape face had begun to slowly, inexorably, sink into itself, like a mental Atlantis. Roadmap lines of laughter were slowly erased, and smoothed, into a serene, macabre mask of hardening shell, beneath which the glimmering light of pleasant thought, and youthful adventure, had long since flown to the Heart's Somewhere Else.

Our eyes connected, and locked, in a breathless
millisecond
of faint, flicker current, while his clicking jut of bones and
drum-skin mocked the twilight, a still-life statement of
itself, in "live" bas relief. He coughed, once, the orbs
rolling back in slot-like measurement, and I was past him,
still holding my breath, and savouring, reverently.......

A "Protection" poem, custom-wise....

…..some kind of miracle, one shovel knocking two people out with a single blow…she should have brought her own, dammit, instead of borrowing his…. Arguing over "shovelling shit" was just too rich, but knocking each other out in the process, was, well—beyond all "scenarios", really. What were the odds?

"Shovel ricochet injury, actually, doc"….he heard himself mumbling the words aloud, in some pristine emergency room, and winced, more from the impossibility of the explanation, (and his embarassment at her old-school methods), than the reality of the soft warmth of a bloodied nose running down the back of his throat—this was SOME STRONG WOMAN! Gingerly, he slid his hand up to feel the soft depression, above the bridge of his nose—apparently the newest example of spontaneous agricultural mask carving (he was afraid to ask any "arts" questions, after that stern, steady, sudden, and extremely unexpected repeated request for response)…the scar would be permanent—and he didn't mind a bit,

Upon reflection—

But he "slap-snapped" out of it,

Knowing she had been

Desperate.

He had been delirious with snow.

The Administrative Years — A retrospective

Rhymes in Time

Longevity…
Brevity…
Duplicity…
Simplicity…
Freneticism…
Asceticism…
Rarity…
Asperity…
The Thunder…
The Wonder…
The history…
The mystery…
The Same…
In a frame…
Avoiding intellectual slavery
With a kind of writer's bravery
So that the mind's eye
Turns a blind eye
To everything this woman could be…
But isn't, in a hug.

Today's Woman

Who is today's woman? Is she you or me?
Is she anyone, that she aspired to be?
Does she cry? Does she laugh? Does she
Sing a note or two?
Who is the woman on the wall? Is she me or you?
Is she a duchess? Is she a maid?
Does she sigh at dues now long since paid?
Does she swing her scarf and scoff
At men who send her flowers,
And dream of kind, sad eyes
During long and quiet hours?
Does she sleep well? Does she pray well?
Are there people quick to stare
At one whose sense of privacy
Shakes decorum and blue hair?
Perhaps she's faded, perhaps she shines
Still, in a place where all women stand;
But, whether jaded or still young,
She links each woman, hand-to-hand.
Are her eyes too filled with tears,
To wade through Time's black, binding chains?
Her strength is of Today, though wearily,
She shoulders the burdens of yesterday's pains.

The College Street Apartment

Musings upon the Wildflowers in the Back Parking Lot

The flowers grow wild, nodding their heads, sleepy in the gloom;
I watch them from my perch on the balcony, feeling a little like Emily, all the while,
Comfortable in the known reaches of my living room,
And dreaming of days, and knights, and wild flowers in still wilder,
Glorious array,
As I scribble and wait, and consider
The coming night's imminent slumber.
I can't help thinking, as those tired flowers slowly fade
until the morn,
If they share my sense of wonder.

Untitled

My heart beats its daily pattern,
Just as yours carries you
From place to place.
The thread that binds us together
Is an intangible link
Between two rhythms that
Keep time separately,
But, silently, sing the same song.

Wind's song

Once again, the sky fades into sleepy time,
And the grass grows wet beneath me
As I wait for your return.
Somehow, the sighing wind must
Carry my thoughts to you,
And the outstretched arms of
The boughs that shelter me
Barely manage to catch
Your reply.

A dog's life

My tiger brindle Brandy is a patient sort of dog,
As she ponderously listens to my literary fog.
She shrugs upon the carpet, and quirks a questioning ear
When I "rave on" about Pinter, in relation to King Lear.

She questions the relationship
With a flop of her thin paw,
As I rhapsodize on Beckett,
And eulogize on Shaw,
And I do think, (though I'm not quite sure; it's often hard to place)
If that stretched-out posture hides a canine yawn
'stead of dog laughs—in my face!

The Renaissance Man

He's a looker, that one; a Real one in every way:
He can build a house, and climb the stairs to gaze in
Fascination, at the Milky Way.
He's a cooker, that one; his recipe for loved involves
A love of song, and the simpler love of Mysteries accepted
and unsolved.
He's a dancer, too; each step can take me to a bit of heaven
And nimble feet tread surely among rocks strewn on the path
where bread is oft' unleaven'd;
For he walks the walk of Freedom,
And talks the talk of Life,
And I, Renaissance Woman,
Am proud to be
His wife.

A Brief Sonata on Interior Decorating, in several movements

Today I moved a couch and chair,
And sought to find a proper place
For each of them, within this room,
Though limited, by time and space.
Bound thus, by simple, sad design
I struggled to perform the task;
And, thinking balance all the time,
The chore was done before the ask!
And so, replete, I sate awhile,
And wondered if I could but write
Of such a feat as this (I smile);
A tiny bit of Art tonight!

"Peas", she said.

These days, I don't much feel like a "sweet pea".
(I feel more like broccoli with a college education.
I always liked it more than cauliflower, anyway—if only
because it smelled better as it got older!)
Give me the shade of a leafy, green tree any day:
I'll hang my laundry on its boughs,
And let the water in the stream nearby
Tickle my toes.
Perhaps the kind hands of the whispering wind
Will dry my hair,
As I stare off into the clouds,
Dreaming of stars…

On carpet deodorizer

Sprinkling much like fairy twinkles, from the jar of
Fortune's Sweet Smells,
The carpet freshener does what it's supposed to do,
And fills the scatter mat
with another
hail
of Chemical "fresh" ness.
The dog seems happy enough,
As she sneezes at "country peach",
Instead of
"simmering roses"…

Watford Days

An afternoon with a winged waif (for Norm and Cindy)

Today, I opened up the door, to see upon the step,
A frightened, shaking, little bird, who'd fallen from his nest.
It waited there, expectantly, as if he knew I'd heard his cry,
And, while I cooed softly to its little face, he sighed, and briefly closed his eyes.
I sat with him, within my perch/porch, safe in the comfort of my favourite chair,
And, while coaxing him to eat a bit, I thought I heard his mother, singing near there.
I was quite careful not to touch, though cradling him in old, soft, cloth, with
The poor thing shuddering all the while, like some poor disoriented moth.
And when his little wings had dried, from the steady, dripping rain,
He fluffed them proudly out, like a bedraggled owl, suddenly, quite right again.
The rain, with time, turned to softer, trickling mist; a soft caress of nature's dew,
And so I placed him in the v-shaped hand of a kindly old branch,
To start his life anew,
(And when he went upon his way, a part of me flew, too!)

Words after a tutoring session

Words.

Words strung.

Words strung together with effort.

Words strung together with effort, like beautiful seeds.

Words strung together with effort, like beautiful seeds on a necklace.

Words strung together with effort, like beautiful seeds on a necklace of a boy.

Words strung together with effort, like beautiful seeds on a necklace of a boy wishing to give something.

Words strung together with effort, like beautiful seeds on a necklace of a boy wishing to give something back.

Words strung together with effort, like beautiful seeds on a necklace of a boy wishing to give something back,

Are the most magnificent of pearls.

The small sentinels

There is a moment, just after twilight,
When the fairies, having spent the day in fairy work
Cheering children who increasingly
Ignore them
Tiredly gather for their daily meal together.
You can see where they hold their little meetings,
For they are shy, these little folks,
And ask the wild lace and clover to give them a canopy
For their times together.
It is a kind of wild, regal splendour, too
For their royalty,
For the fairy people cling to tradition
And they, and the plants,
Hold the king or queen
In very high esteem.
There is music, played in time, and sung from little throats
In tune with the accompaniment of the crickets
And those smaller, gentler birds
Who are often far too willow'-the-wisp
In spirit to shout out their songs in midday,
Like some of their larger cousins.
It's a kind of natural symphony, that ebbs and flows
With the evening light of watchful fireflies,
Keeping time with the hint of breeze
That carries the loving song, with gentle, caressing hands,
To sleepy little ears
As they murmur their children's bed-time prayers,
And say a blessing for
The guardians of their hearts,
The little people.

And I? I am grown, but young enough in heart
To listen, still,
In my chair.

On vegetables (an angry response to elder abuse)

I consider my vegetables with great consternation. There are, after all, so many varieties from which to choose…

Part one: Potatoes

Potatoes, with their magnetic, silly eyes, and lovable earthiness,
Are staples.
Yet, they become a veritable culinary masterpiece,
With imagination.

Part two: Zucchini

Too much water, some say;
Better to toss them into soup, or casseroles, or something
That merely benefits, in bulk, from the addition of
This speckled and seedy delight.
And yet…by themselves, with a slight addition
The wonders of spices, and the tartness of old cheese,
Their delicacy of flavour
Needs no mask.

Part three: Broccoli

Such colour! Such witty, wonderfully shaped, stalwart appeal!
A stalk of this vegetable tree brightens up a dull plate.
One can imagine a saucy jacket, and its comforting effect,
And dream—rather romantically—of cheerful broccoli
Waving its branches through another sparkling and witty
Dinner hour.

<u>Part four: Cauliflower</u>

Like some huge vegetable brain, each firm flowerette extends
To its consumer, an invitation to enjoy the crunchy buds of
Good nutrition.
Blossoming ideas are only a part of its parts,
Although, if left too long alone, it rather
Smells!......

Creative Cover letters I really wanted to send

The Fashion Funhouse
for Veterans
You Buy, We Ply (you with requests to buy more)

Dear Owner and Displayer,

I really need a part-time job, but I look rather bad in nouvea-bandage. The only time was when I was four, and I dumped a pot of spaghetti water on my little sister and I. We had matching arm splotches for a week, but somehow I never thought it would ever become a fashion statement…the first aid thing, I mean. Mine got kind of yucky because I played outside in the sandbox, while wearing it, and wow! Did I catch heck for that…whew!

Anyway, everyone kind of had this slightly breathless, worried expression on their faces, and, well, if I was a customer, I'd be afraid of sudden attacks of strange bugs, or confused ambulance guys, responding, or something. Everyone sort of ducked, and looked, before they talked to you. Is that normal, in your store?

I really have to tell you, nicely: the clothes scared me, you scared me, and you really should do something about that guy who stands in the corner and thanks everyone for not stepping on him. I really think that that is taking secure politeness a BIT too far, don't you? He's liable to get hurt, what with people's short tempers, these days. Besides, one rather short-sighted old bird kept trying to wipe his feet on the poor little man's toupee….

Just thought I'd tell you. I really want the job, though. I can do gauze for anything, other than just commission (which really isn't fair, you know)—but I wear cotton underwear, okay?

Yours truly,

Marva Lous.

November 24, 199?

Mrs. Winny Loudly
Number twelve, Large Feet Close
Neighbourly, Quanset

re: interview, bingley's bangles

Dear Miss Loudly:

I just had to write and apologize to you, regarding my recent interview.

I was appalled that you saw me in such a sorry state, but I'd missed the bus, and the only one was four blocks down. I ran to get the transfer, and my shoe caught in one of those round things in the street. Well, you can imagine; my heel stayed, my foot went, and so did I—down for the count, in front of a passing hotdog cart, which just managed to splash me enough to firmly freeze the hairspray I'd used into a sheet-like effect. I know I looked rather like a kind of odd, barking kite when I arrived, but I'd only been able to get a standing place on the bus, and the darned window was open, despite the sleet….well, you can guess the rest, I expect.

I am not, (contrary to what the one saleslady mentioned, somewhat scathingly, I thought) "practicing football camouflage eye rouge techniques"; the frankfurther cart let loose quite a flood of icy, muddy puddle business, and I admit I did buy the mascara on sale…..sigh. Really, I did have one of those awful plastic rain hat things, but I dropped it in the puddle, and the cart went over it, along with my hand—which was why I screamed, when you shook it. I do apologize; at the time I hadn't realized I'd broken anything, I was so anxious to get there on time—which I DID manage to do, after all; HURRAH!

I'm afraid I didn't manage to catch the name of the saleslady who had been standing with you, at the time. She rather reminded me of a slinky…quite, ah…. CHEERFUL sounding, if a bit critical. Of course, I already had a TEENSY bit of a headache BEFORE I arrived at the store….

Ah, well, no matter; it's a lovely shop, Miss Proudly, and I can see how you'd be loud in it.

I am so hoping you'll call me....by my PROPER name....er, on the telephone, if you wouldn't mind, if somewhat more quietly....ahem.

Thanks again for your absolutely impeccable manners; I expect that you'll be sending me a bill for the front carpet, but, if not, then just being able to replace it with my own jingling would be pleasure enough in itself. Cough. I may have looked a tad disshevelled at the time, but, truly, I'd sell more bangles than you could shake a stick at.

Oh, dear, I do fear that I'm gushing a bit, at this point, but I did so want you to know that the construction gentleman kindly informed me that new tar often lifts right out of broadloom, if you but scrub a bit, without smearing, he said.

Hoping to speak with you at your earliest convenience,

I remain,

Your faithful applicant,

Alpeeta Dudley.

sign posted on tree with small axe

BIGGALL'S WIGGLES
(fISH LURES AND CURIO ITEMS FOR THE
FISHERMAN AND HIS FAMILY)
tIRD LAKE FROM TA LEFT OF SNONKER'S
BOATHOUSE
SQUEAKED IN, ONTARIO

HEY, YAS! I JUS' HAD TO RITE YAS AND LET YAS NO
DAT DA ONE STEP UP NEAR 'TA FRONT
IS DERN NEAR A KILLER. ME AND MA WENT TO
BUY ONE OF 'EM LITTLE SPECKLED LOORS
WHAT LOOK LIKE PUMPERNICKEL LOAVES
(HERE DEY'RE A REAL TREAT FOR DA MUSKEY),
AND'TA 'TING JES SEEMED TO LOOM OUT OF
NOWWAIRS, TO CAUSE ME GREAT PERSONAL PAIN. MIND YA',
I BOUNCED A BIT, WHAT WIT' DA WEATHER BEIN' COLD, AND
THE WISER'S
BEING WAR, 'N ALL, BUT STILL, YOU SHOULD
REALLY MEBBE PUT A FLASHIN' SIGHN NEAR DA
BIG PINE ON DA LEFT, WHAT TO WARN PEOPLE
WITH, LIKE.

JESS BEIN' A CONCERNET CITIZEN. aLSO, I
LOST MY HAIRPIECE, WHAT MA GOT ME, TREE
CHRISTMASSES BACK, AND IT SORTA' FEELS
LIKE A LONG TRIP ON A COLD NIGHT, IF YAS
KNOW WHAT I MEAN, GETTIN' PERSONAL, LIKE.

sincerely, THE FIDDLIN'S, OVER NEAR TA OLD ROCK JUT.

Uninspired

I watch the words drip from my fingers, like the rain I had been waiting for,
After some terrible crop drought.
I keep shaking them, willing the words to somehow
elongate out of them, like silly putty,
when you fling it around,
Or spaghetti tests, aimed at the ceiling—great timeless
judging methods of quality cooking;
But
The page still seems like some bland tea towel, tattered, which I continue
to wring into
Craft-like paper twists of impatience, at my own
Silent testimony to the ongoing
battle with
My hands.

A Knight Returns (A Poem for old Lovers)

Oh, dear; I've dropped my pen again, and with it,
One more quiet thought: There now!
I've got it back again, so; on to more enticing rot.
(Oh dear! I've blobbed a new ink spot.)
Well, keep on trying, some dear soul said;
(But all these blobs confuse my head!
I think I'll have some tea, instead.)
Well, darn! The burner's not quite red;
Perhaps I'll check it with my hand…
GOOD GRIEF! You think that I would understand
That fire is hot, and stalling's rot!
I think I'll just clean up that spot…but wait!
I've left my tea behind;
(Perhaps I'll need it, to unwind—)
I'll just go fix another kind.
Well, now; I never noticed, after all,
The rug, upturned, that broke my fall.
(I should have placed it in the hall.)
Well, back to my dear cup, now, I should think;
Oh, dear! I've knocked it in the sink…
AND that daring, naughty shade of pink…
Sigh…Oh well; I'll get the glue;
I'm sure that only one or two more pieces—THERE!
I've STEPPED on that one! PHEW!
WHAT on earth is that odd smell?
The KETTLE's boiled down to the PAINT!
Oh, dear; good grief; oh….BLOODY HELL!
I s'pose it's only just as well;
At least no one has rung…..THE BELL!
SO, HERE I STAND, CRACKED CUP IN HAND,

THE KETTLE SHRIEKING MADLY ON THE STAND;
It's prob 'ly just some silly….MAN!
I think that I'll just set this down
And try my best to hide my frown
Despite the fact the pink's gone brown
(Iboughtthisgluelastyearintown)
Now WHO, I wonder, COULD that be?
(No one thinks to visit me:)
I daren't think.NO! Not him!Not HE!
Oh, DARLING! Finally!…..company!

Come in; I've just been making tea….
Eh? What's that nonsense about "we"?
OH!That…..Well….go ahead and call me Dee.
We still can THINK on it…HEE HEE…
(Oh, hell; I'm only eighty-three!)
NOW DON'T YOU START WITH "come, sweet pea"!
At our age, dear, it's heresy;
I've long forgot love's victory.
OH! WATCH THE RUG, NOW!….It sticks up;
I thought….oooh! You're like some love-crazed pup!
…..It's up the stairs, and to the right;
(I hope we don't expire tonight…)
Oh well! We'll go down with a fight…
You've brought a THINGY!
Well…..GOOD KNIGHT!

978-0-595-35176-3
0-595-35176-X

Printed in the United States
28680LVS00001B/520-552